Hi, I'm
NORMAN

The Story of American Illustrator
NORMAN ROCKWELL

Written by
ROBERT BURLEIGH

Illustrated by
WENDELL MINOR

A Paula Wiseman Book
SIMON & SCHUSTER BOOKS FOR YOUNG READERS
New York London Toronto Sydney New Delhi

ACKNOWLEDGMENTS

Special thanks to Deputy Director and Chief Curator Stephanie Plunkett and Archivist Venus Van Ness at the Norman Rockwell Museum for their assistance and consultation in the development of this book.

SIMON & SCHUSTER BOOKS FOR YOUNG READERS
An imprint of Simon & Schuster Children's Publishing Division
1230 Avenue of the Americas, New York, New York 10020
Text copyright © 2019 by Robert Burleigh
Illustrations copyright © 2019 by Wendell Minor
All rights reserved, including the right of reproduction in whole or in part in any form.
SIMON & SCHUSTER BOOKS FOR YOUNG READERS is a trademark of Simon & Schuster, Inc.
For information about special discounts for bulk purchases, please contact Simon & Schuster Special Sales at 1-866-506-1949 or business@simonandschuster.com.
The Simon & Schuster Speakers Bureau can bring authors to your live event. For more information or to book an event, contact the Simon & Schuster Speakers Bureau at 1-866-248-3049 or visit our website at www.simonspeakers.com.
Book design by Laurent Linn
The text for this book was set in Cantoria MT Std.
The illustrations for this book are rendered in watercolor, gouache, and pencil.
Manufactured in China
0719 SCP
First Edition
10 9 8 7 6 5 4 3 2 1
Library of Congress Cataloging-in-Publication Data
Names: Burleigh, Robert, author. | Minor, Wendell, illustrator.
Title: Hi, I'm Norman : the story of American illustrator Norman Rockwell / Robert Burleigh ; illustrated by Wendell Minor.
Description: New York : Simon & Schuster Books for Young Readers, [2019] | "A Paula Wiseman book." | Audience: Ages 4–8. | Audience: K to Grade 3.
Identifiers: LCCN 2018040503| ISBN 9781442496705 (hardcover) | ISBN 9781442496712 (eBook)
Subjects: LCSH: Rockwell, Norman, 1894–1978—Juvenile literature. | Artists—United States—Biography—Juvenile literature.
Classification: LCC ND237.R68 B87 2019 | DDC 759.13 [B]—dc23
LC record available at https://lccn.loc.gov/2018040503

For Paula Wiseman, editor and friend
—R. B.

To the Rockwell Family
—W. M.

Hi, I'm Norman. Norman Rockwell. Come on in.

This is my studio. Here's the easel where I paint, and there are the paints, the brushes, my chair, and the walls hung with sketches—you name it.

I love it here. Every artist loves being in the studio. I close the door behind me and enter my own special world. Because art is my life and has been for as long as I can remember.

Of course, I haven't always had a nice studio like this one. No, not at all.

There I am—a little kid—after dinner at the dining room table, drawing, while my dad reads me *David Copperfield*. I loved listening to his calm, soft voice. Slowly, the characters came alive in my mind.

Does that ever happen to you?

I bent forward, biting my lip, erasing and starting again, until I captured the people and the scenes I heard there on the paper in front of me.

Even way back then I loved telling stories with pictures—and I still do.

But our dining room wasn't my only "studio" in those days. Sometimes I had a much bigger one—

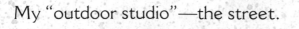

My "outdoor studio"—the street.

I wasn't much of a ball player, but when I drew, things changed. The guys in the neighborhood liked me.

"Draw us a picture, Norm."

I'd grab a piece of chalk from my pocket, kneel down on the sidewalk, and before you knew it, there was a picture of a big lion's head, or one of Admiral Dewey's battleships, or maybe a fire truck being pulled by horses.

Everyone would yell: "Look at that!" "Do one more!"

The truth is, my ability was just something I had, like the color of my hair or eyes. My older brother, Jarvis, could jump over three orange crates. Me, I could draw.

Oh, I nearly forgot. Grade school. I'll be the first to confess that I wasn't all that good at paying attention. But drawing was different. And lucky for me, my favorite teacher gave me lots of opportunity.

I sometimes filled the whole blackboard with holiday scenes or pictures of covered wagons rumbling toward a far-off snow-capped mountain.

I admit I was pretty darn proud when Miss Smith said with a smile, "Norman's drawn something we've been reading about: settlers heading west on the Oregon Trail."

My classmates let out a big "Ooooohhhhh."

That was great to hear—but art school, a few years later, wasn't always as easy.

I can still picture the room where the art students worked: the gray light drifting down through the skylights, the smudged walls, and the floors littered with rags and hardened paint. But who cared? If you love something, you take the bad with it too, right?

I still remember things my teachers told me:

"Step over the frame, Norman, and live in the picture."

"Feel a picture hard, Rockwell, and the public will feel it the same way."

Now and then my favorite instructor would walk by and "correct" my drawing by scrawling a big, thick charcoal line through something I thought was perfect. Ouch—that hurt!

But I listened, learned, and got better and better. I even won a prize in illustration class.

You might say I entered art school raw—and came out cooked.

It was time to test myself in the real world, and believe me—I wanted to pass the test. There wasn't a job I wouldn't accept.

I drew Santas and angels for Christmas booklets. I drew body parts for medical texts. I illustrated a children's book too. I was a young struggling artist, and every smidgen helped.

Whatever I did, I did my best. I painted "100%" in gold at the top of my easel. Every time I began a picture, I was determined that it would be perfect.

Funny, but I sometimes felt I was chasing and at the same time being chased. Chasing my dream of becoming a great artist. But also being chased by the fear that I wasn't good enough.

Was I? I was twenty-two years old, and ready or not, I decided to find out.

The *Saturday Evening Post* was the most popular magazine in America. And every week an artist had his or her illustration—a "picture-story"—smack dab on the cover.

I decided to go to the *Post*'s office. I remember sitting and fidgeting in the waiting room while the editor was inside, looking over a few of my pictures. Was I nervous? Are you kidding? My heart was pounding like a sledgehammer.

Finally the door swung open—and out came Mr. Dower. I was almost afraid to look up.

"We'll take *all five* of these," he said simply. I just gulped. For a moment I couldn't find any words—I was that overjoyed. My paintings—on the cover of the *Saturday Evening Post*.

And $75 for each one. Wow!

Over the years, I did 300-plus covers for the *Post*, which is a lot of ideas to come up with. And doing covers is doubly hard because a cover has to tell the *whole* story in *one* picture. And the viewer has to get it—at first glance. Bingo—just like that.

How do I get ideas? Well, I doodle. Ever try it? It's my way of brainstorming. I let my mind wander as I scratch out funny little pictures, one after the other. Maybe up comes a dog. Then a bit later, perhaps a person—a hungry man. Then after some more pictures, the dog is chasing him. Hmmmm. More doodling. Perhaps the man is carrying something the dog wants. What could it be?

Hey, it's a fresh-baked pie. Now I see it. The picture-story: A tramp is running away, carrying a pie he has just stolen, and a hungry pup is barking after him. Arf, arf!

In fact, that's one of my *Post* covers. I called it—guess what?—*Dog Biting Man in Seat of Pants.*

Before I start my painting, I always set up the whole scene to look just as it will in the final picture. I search hard for my models, too.

Adult models, and even kid models, are fairly easy. At least you can talk to them!

But how about animals? Some sure can be tough to persuade.

I even used a turkey model once. It didn't seem to know it was destined for stardom. It hopped from the model stand and fluttered around the room, flapping its wings and snapping its beak until it settled down. I hid behind some crates till the coast was clear, wondering if I should have been an animal trainer instead of an artist!

But I told myself I was an artist. And I finished the painting at last.

Then, suddenly, I was famous.

People saw *themselves* in my pictures. I portrayed average people, everyday Americans, sometimes happy or sometimes confronting life's little problems, but always with a bit of humor. What did I paint? Just simple things:

A grandfather laughing at this look-alike snowman.

A schoolgirl waiting outside the principal's office.

A boy and girl watching the moon.

A scrawny teenager lifting weights.

But no matter what I painted, I was always trying to show how *I* saw the world.

The truth is, I couldn't paint ugliness. I suppose I painted life like I'd like it to be. As I grew up, I found the world wasn't always a pleasant place. So I decided that even though life wasn't perfect, I'd paint only the ideal aspects of it. That way, my pictures showed the best side of things.

But what should an artist do when war comes?

Well, *I* volunteered. I was too old to fight, but I fought with the one weapon I had—my art.

I made four paintings and called them *The Four Freedoms*, based on a speech President Franklin D. Roosevelt gave during World War II. I wanted to show what we were fighting for—freedom of speech and worship, and freedom from want and fear. The paintings were exhibited around the country and helped bring in millions of dollars in war bonds.

Once I went up with a squad of paratroopers in training. Talk about courage! I watched them leap out, one by one, from the plane's doorway and into the blue sky as their chutes bloomed open. "Geronimo!" I had to sketch fast, too, but I got it all. Hey, I wasn't called "the kid with the camera eye" for nothing!

The war was finally over. The world was changing.
Could I change too?
My country was struggling with a new issue: freedom for all, white folk *and* black. People protested, people marched, people died for their beliefs.

My large painting *The Problem We All Live With* was my answer. A little black girl in a bright dress walks bravely between four US marshals. She is entering an all-white school for the first time. On the wall behind her are ugly, hate-filled words, and the red splash from a thrown tomato.

I wanted my painting to match the power of the moment. I sketched out my idea and had photos taken of several models.

But then I hesitated. Would this subject, I wondered, go with all my earlier, happier ones?

I told myself: If you believe it, Norm, paint it.

And the picture got done.

Well, time to get to work. I love looking ahead—because every painting I make is a new adventure.

That's me, by the way, in the picture I'm just starting on the easel. I'm wrapping a ribbon around America's Liberty Bell. I even use myself as a model now and then. Why not? Saves time—and money. And sometimes, I just like looking out at viewers from the picture side of the canvas!

But I like looking back, too—back over my life. When I do, I seem to hear distant voices calling to me: "Draw us a picture, Norm."

I hear my dad calling.

I hear my pals in the old neighborhood calling.

I hear my classmates calling.

I hear the editors at the *Post* calling.

I hear America calling.

"Draw us a picture, Norm."

And you know what? I always did.

Norman Rockwell

was probably America's best-known artist during the middle years of the twentieth century. But who was Norman Rockwell?

Put simply and plainly, Norman was first of all an *artist*. From an early age he dedicated himself to making art. And during his long life-time (1894–1978) he did just that. Over his working years Rockwell produced more than four thousand original works—paintings, draw-ings, illustrations, portraits, book covers, and magazine covers. (He painted more than 320 covers for the *Saturday Evening Post* alone.) But even so, he once said, "I'll never have enough time to paint all the pictures I'd like to." And he meant it.

That's because his subject was large—America itself, in all its many aspects: happy, sad, funny, heroic, historic, and more. From holiday celebrations and quiet family moments, to peaceful city scenes or the struggles of men, women, and children to make the world, and the United States, a safer and more just place—Norman Rockwell was ready with pencil, pen, or paintbrush in hand. "Every new picture is a new adventure," he liked to say. "The secret is not to look back."

Norman began his career in the early 1900s, a time of some radio broadcasts, a few movies, and no television. Most Americans got their "visual" information from magazines, often from popular magazines such as the weekly *Saturday Evening Post*, where young Norman's art often appeared before a large audience—one that would only grow over the coming years.

His magazine cover paintings (and all of his works) showed his great skill in presenting colorful, realistic scenes full of average people, and the ideas for the cover pictures came from Norman himself. "The first job is to hit on a good idea," he said. But how to begin? It was no easy task, and he spent twelve or more hours in his studio almost every day of the week. "I retire to a quiet room with a supply of cheap paper and sharp pencils." The idea was just the beginning of a complicated process. In addition to collecting many reference photographs, he would find models and sketch his idea in more detail, drawing and redrawing before finally painting, always aiming to get a "whole story" into one work of art. "I guess I am a storyteller," he once said.

During Norman's lifetime, American art began to change. Abstract art, surrealist art, and other new styles of painting emerged in the twentieth century. The subject matter of many artists became bolder, too. But Norman had already found his subject and his style. He stayed true to his vision, always continuing to work. "Maybe as I grew up and found that the world wasn't the perfectly pleasant place I had thought it to be, I unconsciously decided that, even if it wasn't an ideal world, it should be. I paint life like I would like it to be."

Norman had three children: Jarvis, Thomas, and Peter. Although he liked nothing more than to be near (and especially in) his studio, he sometimes traveled to Europe, or to Hollywood, where he painted portraits of a few movie stars! In his later years he did portraits of several American presidents, and a number of highly regarded paintings dealing with civil rights. Norman could make fun of himself too. When he was older, in the midst of a long career that was still going strong, he remarked, "Some people think I painted Lincoln from life, but I haven't been around that long. Not quite." As his fame continued to grow, he became in many people's eyes the symbol of a great artist. Although he sometimes modestly proclaimed that he "wasn't an artist, but only an illustrator," he also said, "The great band of illustrators have shown us to ourselves and I am proud to be among their company."

Norman Rockwell's work is now in many major museums, and one museum—the Norman Rockwell Museum in Stockbridge, Massachusetts—is devoted entirely to his life and work. His drawings and paintings are increasingly sought out, his pronouncements on art are often quoted, and the prices for his work continue to rise.

There are many more interesting things to say about Norman Rockwell, but one thing we may be sure of: The art of Norman Rockwell will be with us for a long time to come.

AUTHOR'S NOTE

NORMAN AND ME!

In Norman Rockwell's 1938 oil painting titled *The Deadline* (sometimes called *Blank Canvas*), done for a *Saturday Evening Post* cover, an artist (presumably Rockwell) sits on a swivel chair in front of a more or less empty canvas, scratching his head. *Where do I start? Where do I go from here?*

I had a similar feeling myself when I began to write what has become *Hi, I'm Norman*. Why? Because writing about Norman Rockwell is a bit like writing a history of twentieth-century America. He came of age at a time when pictures were worth a thousand words. And his amazingly descriptive pictures told stories that brought people together, illustrating common values spiced with a uniquely American humor. His life and work extended well over half a century, encompassing major events that shaped the American consciousness. And his paintings reflected many of those changes.

That's why I finally decided that the best person to tell Rockwell's story was Rockwell himself. But first I had to learn about Norman's life!

I loved discovering how this unathletic young boy entertained his rowdier friends with his amazing drawing ability. I loved seeing how he worked through his uncertainties about his life and work. I loved learning how Rockwell kept working, day after day in his studio, to make his paintings. And I loved the fact that Rockwell, always the patriot, made important works of art, during World War II and later, that celebrated the civil rights of every American citizen.

Norman Rockwell's story is an intriguing, inspiring American story—and I enjoyed telling it.

I'd like to add my gratitude to three people who helped in the writing of this book. First, tremendous thanks to my friend and longtime co-creator, the artist Wendell Minor, whose beautiful paintings ignite this entire book. Second, thanks to Stephanie Plunkett, deputy director and chief curator at the Norman Rockwell Museum. And finally, many thanks to my friend and editor at Simon & Schuster, Paula Wiseman, ever ready with key suggestions and a helping hand.

And of course—a great big hurrah for the artist himself, America's one and only Norman Rockwell!

—*Robert Burleigh*

ILLUSTRATOR'S NOTE

I have admired Norman Rockwell's art since I was a boy growing up in Illinois. I would look for the latest edition of the *Saturday Evening Post* at our local drugstore newsstand, always keeping an eye out for a Rockwell cover. Those covers had a profound effect on me and my desire to become an artist. Rockwell's ability to tell a whole story in one picture truly amazed me, and I credit the power of those pictures with inspiring me to become an illustrator.

It is my sincerest hope that *Hi, I'm Norman* will introduce Norman Rockwell's story and art to a new generation of admirers and perhaps inspire others. Robert Burleigh has done a masterful job in imagining Norman speaking to the reader in the first person, bringing the artist to life in a very personal way.

As an illustrator I have to say that it was most humbling to create art for this book. In fact, that is an understatement. Norman Rockwell's art is so unique that it is instantly recognizable. Trying to emulate his style would be impossible. Therefore, I have done my best to tell Rockwell's story in my style, with apologies to Norman, of course.

For securing the rights to Rockwell's paintings, I would like to thank Margaret Rockwell of the Norman Rockwell Family Agency, Cris Piquinela at Curtis Publishing Company/the *Saturday Evening Post*, and Mike Mueller of IMG Licensing Worldwide. For their support and encouragement for the book *Hi, I'm Norman: The Story of American Illustrator Norman Rockwell*, many thanks to Norman Rockwell Museum staff Laurie Norton Moffatt, director and CEO; Stephanie Haboush Plunkett, deputy director and chief curator; and Venus Van Ness, archivist.

—*Wendell Minor*

Some of the paintings in the book are rendered by
Wendell Minor and represent works of Norman Rockwell.
They are listed below in book order.

(All painting titles are per the Norman Rockwell Museum collection and archive.)

Cover: *Triple Self-Portrait*—Saturday Evening Post cover, February 13, 1960

"Hi, I'm Norman.": *Springtime: Boy and Rabbit*—Saturday Evening Post cover, April 27, 1935

"Hi, I'm Norman." (facing page): *Waiting for the Art Editor*—Unpublished *Saturday Evening Post* cover, circa 1970

"But I listened, learned, and got better and better.": Student illustration at age seventeen, awarded the Thomas Fogarty Illustration Award

"It was time to test myself in the real world . . ." (facing page): *Boy Skating*—*Boys' Life*, January 1914

"Finally the door swung open . . .": *Boy with Baby Carriage*—Saturday Evening Post cover, May 20, 1916

"Finally the door swung open . . .": *Gramps at the Plate*—Saturday Evening Post cover, August 5, 1916

"Hey, it's a fresh-baked pie.": *Dog Biting Man in Seat of Pants*—Saturday Evening Post cover, August 18, 1928

"But how about animals?": *Cousin Reginald Catches the Thanksgiving Turkey*—*Country Gentleman*, December 1, 1917

"Then, suddenly, I was famous.": *Grandfather and Snowman*—Saturday Evening Post cover, December 20, 1919

"Then, suddenly, I was famous.": *The Young Lady with the Shiner*—Saturday Evening Post cover, May 23, 1953

"A boy and girl watching the moon.": *Boy and Girl Gazing at Moon*—Saturday Evening Post cover, April 24, 1926

"A boy and girl watching the moon.": *Be a Man*—Saturday Evening Post cover, April 29, 1922

"Well, I volunteered.": *Four Freedoms* posters: 1943 (four million posters), *Freedom of Speech*, *Freedom of Worship*, *Freedom from Want*, *Freedom from Fear* (These paintings were originally published in the *Saturday Evening Post*.)

"I wanted my painting to match the power of the moment.": *The Problem We All Live With*—*Look* magazine, January 14, 1964

"I hear my dad calling.": *Liberty Bell*—*American Artist* magazine, July 1976

SOME IMPORTANT DATES
IN THE LIFE OF NORMAN ROCKWELL

1894   Normal Rockwell is born in New York City on February 3.

1910   Drops out of high school and begins to study art at the National Academy of Design in New York.

1910   Paints first commission, a group of Christmas cards.

1916   Paints first of 322 covers for the *Saturday Evening Post*. His first cover is *Boy with Baby Carriage* (May 20, 1916), and children continue to be a favorite subject in the years to come.

1916   Marries Irene O'Connor. (They divorce in 1930.)

1930   Marries Mary Barstow. The couple eventually has three sons: Jarvis, Thomas, and Peter.

1939   Family moves to Arlington, Vermont.

1943   Rockwell paints four of his most famous paintings, the *Four Freedoms*.

1943   Fire destroys Rockwell's studio in Arlington. However, he rebuilds and carries on.

1953   Family moves to Stockbridge, Massachusetts.

1959   Rockwell's second wife, Mary Barstow Rockwell, dies.

1960   Rockwell's autobiography, *My Adventures As an Illustrator*, is published.

1961   Marries Molly Punderson, a retired school teacher.

1964   Begins to illustrate interior stories for *Look* magazine, where he starts to deal with some of his deeper interests, such as civil rights and the exploration of space.

1973   Establishes a trust that later becomes today's Norman Rockwell Museum in Stockbridge.

1977   Receives America's highest civilian honor, the Presidential Medal of Freedom.

1978   Norman Rockwell dies in Stockbridge on November 8.

Checkers (1928)

Rockwell didn't just illustrate magazine covers. Sometimes, as with *Checkers* (1928), he illustrated magazine stories. This painting is an excellent example of Rockwell's colorful, sharp-eyed illustrations, which tell a story all by themselves. A circus clown and other circus workers are taking a break, playing a game of checkers. It appears from the clown's smile and outstretched hand that he has just driven his opponent (the man in black gazing at the checkerboard) into a difficult position. That's all, my friend. Game over!

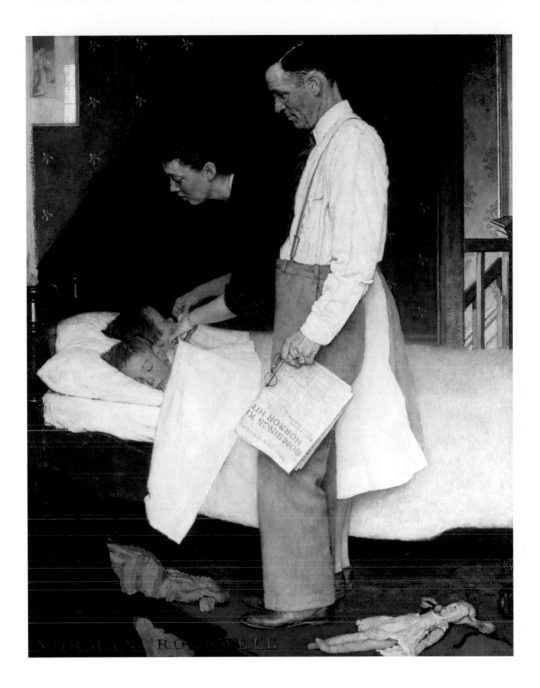

Freedom from Fear (1943)

This was painted in 1943, during World War II, and is one of four of Rockwell's most famous paintings. The only indicator in the painting that the war has started is a newspaper headline. The other three paintings in this series were *Freedom from Want*, *Freedom of Worship*, and *Freedom of Speech*. These are the four freedoms that President Roosevelt had named as reasons for America's decision to enter the war. Here two parents lean over their sleeping children in a quiet and peaceful bedroom. The posters made from these paintings were used to sell bonds that provided large sums of money for the war effort.

Art Critic (1955)

Perhaps Rockwell painted *Art Critic* to respond to some critics who had attacked his work as old-fashioned. (Despite this criticism, he admired many modern painters and had some copies of their work on his studio walls.) The humor here turns on two facts. First the critic, bending over with a magnifying glass, seems to be "analyzing" only a tiny bit of the whole painting. At the same time the female subject of the painting seems to be glancing down and laughing at the critic.

The Problem We All Live With (1964)

Perhaps the most well-known of all Rockwell's paintings, this depicts a young African American girl (Ruby Bridges) being escorted to an all-white school by a group of government agents. Why? In the racially segregated United States of the time, black children were kept out of many (all-white) schools because of local laws or the threat of violence. When the federal government at last intervened, young black students often had to be escorted into the schools past angry white mobs.

Liberty Bell (1976)

Liberty Bell was a painting created for the cover of *American Artist* magazine, celebrating our country's 200th birthday. It was Norman Rockwell's last published work. He passed away two years later in 1978.

SOME ADDITIONAL SOURCES OF INFORMATION ABOUT NORMAN ROCKWELL

If you look up "Norman Rockwell" online or in the library,
you will find a large number of references, articles, and pictures
that cover Rockwell's life, his thoughts, and his work.

Many books deal with Rockwell too. A few of them are:

Claridge, Laura. *Norman Rockwell: A Life.* New York: Random House, 2001.

Gherman, Beverly. *Norman Rockwell: Storyteller with a Brush.* New York: Atheneum Books for Young Readers, 2000.

Guptill, Arthur L. *Norman Rockwell: Illustrator.* New York: Watson-Guptill Publications, 1946.

Haboush Plunkett, Stephanie, and James Kimble. *Enduring Ideals: Rockwell, Roosevelt & the Four Freedoms.* New York: Abbeville Press, 2018.

Pero, Linda Szekely. *American Chronicles: The Art of Norman Rockwell.* Stockbridge, MA: Norman Rockwell Museum, 2007.

Rivoli, Kevin. *In Search of Norman Rockwell's America.* New York: Howard Books, 2008.

Rockwell, Norman. *Norman Rockwell: My Adventures as an Illustrator.* New York: Abrams Books, 1988.

Schick, Ron. *Norman Rockwell: Behind the Camera.* New York: Little, Brown and Co., 2009.

Venezia, Mike. *Norman Rockwell.* New York: Children's Press, 2000.

SOME QUOTES FROM NORMAN ROCKWELL

**These quotes are taken from his autobiography,
My Adventures as an Illustrator by Norman Rockwell.**

"The story of my life is, really, the story of my pictures and how I made them." (13)

"Every artist has his own peculiar way of looking at life." (34)

"I know I'm not satisfied with my work. But that keeps me working." (35)

"I've always wanted to be an artist. I drew, then I found I liked to draw,
and finally I found that I didn't want to do anything else." (37)